FOREVER OURS

JO WALKER
ILLUSTRATED BY
SARA JO FLOYD

Copyright © 2024 Jo Walker

All rights reserved
Second Edition

PAGE PUBLISHING, INC.
CONNEAUT LAKE, PA

First published by Page Publishing 2021

ISBN 979-8-89315-261-6 (CASEBOUND)
ISBN 978-1-64701-396-7 (DIGITAL)

Printed in the United States of America

No part of this book may be reproduced or transmitted in any form or by any means, electronic or mechanical, including photocopying, recording or by an information storage and retrieval system – except by a reviewer who may quote brief passages in a review to be printed in a magazine, newspaper, or on the Web – without permission in writing from the author.

FOREVER OURS

JO WALKER
ILLUSTRATED BY
SARA JO FLOYD

One night when I was very small,
I felt alone and scared;
I cried and cried but no one came,
it seemed like no one cared.

As the days went by and I grew and grew,
I longed for something new;
I didn't know what was missing
and I didn't know what to do.

Until one day something changed when I felt a warm embrace;
It hugged me tight both day and night, but yet I saw no face.

I didn't know what was happening
or why I felt so loved,
or why I seemed to hear these words,
beautiful, *worthy* and *our beloved.*

Little did I know that across the sea,
in a land so far away;
A family was there, on their knees in prayer,
for my protection and care each day.

And then one morning out of the blue
while playing with friends inside,
two people came in and called my name
with their arms stretched open wide.

My heart started racing as I stood in fear,
I didn't know who they were;
I clung to the door as I heard these words:
"This little one is her."

Right at that moment they both plopped on the floor
bringing pictures, toys and more;
They drew me in with all things new,
there was so much to explore.

Then something happened as they held me near,
a feeling I never felt before;
I just knew they were mine, that I now belonged
and an orphan I was no more.

We climbed on a plane and flew for miles,
I didn't know what to think;
But as they held me tight, my heart rejoiced,
it had found its missing link.

Once safe on the ground we walked through some doors,
when I saw the perfect sight;
They ran with great speed and embraced me with glee
and squeezed my neck so tight.

"WELCOME HOME" they yelled with great delight,
both beaming from ear to ear;
We have been waiting so long to see your sweet face
and now you're finally HERE!

As we jumped in the car and made our way home
with my siblings singing a song,
they held my hands and made me laugh,
how great to finally belong!

Once we made it home there was much to enjoy,
new toys and clothes to see;
I couldn't believe they loved me so much
that they would do this all for me.

But as night drew near and it was time for bed
my heart racing and feeling scared;
my mama stayed close and held me tight,
I just knew she really cared.

She started singing songs that I didn't know
as she rocked me from left to right;
Then she whispered the words I'd heard before,
when alone in the orphanage at night.

"You are beautiful, worthy and our beloved,
fearfully and wonderfully made;
You are safe here with us and you will forever be ours,
you're the answer to the prayers we've prayed."

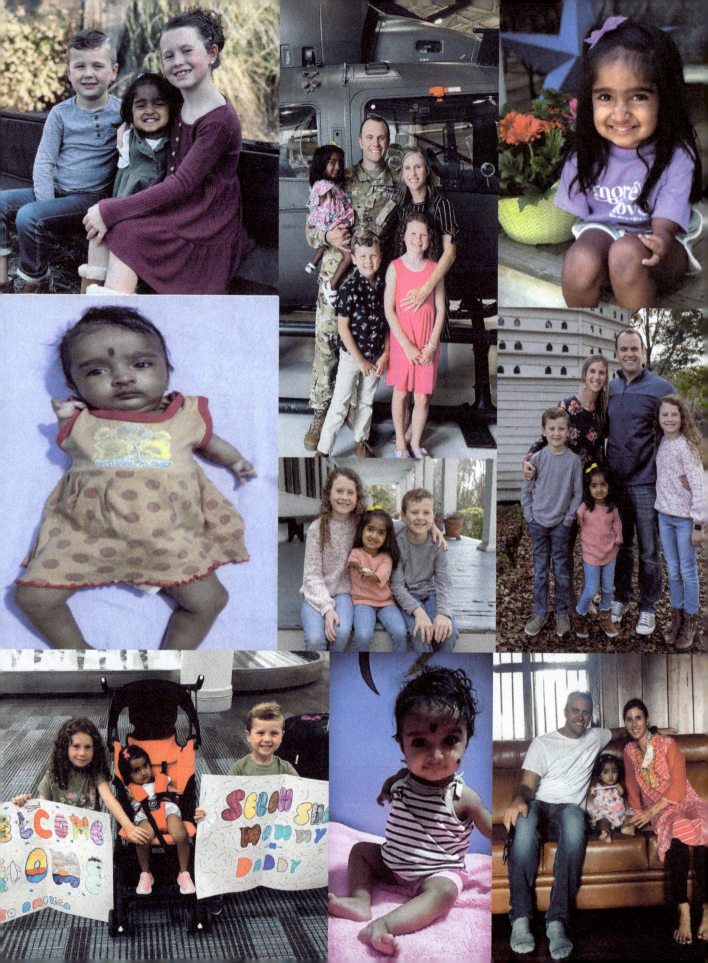

About SHANI

THIS BOOK IS DEDICATED TO OUR THREE BEAUTIFUL CHILDREN. In 2017, the Lord called us to consider adoption and in 2021 we were matched with our beautiful Indian princess. Although Shani was born with limb difference in both arms and scoliosis of the spine, she lets nothing hold her back. She is so incredibly smart, funny, motivated and extremely determined to succeed at anything she puts her mind to. Her life has been such a blessing to us and we are so thankful for the opportunity to love her forever.

About the AUTHOR

JO WALKER WAS BORN IN BLOEMFONTEIN, SOUTH AFRICA, and now resides in South Carolina. She has a bachelor's degree from Old Dominion University, a diploma in women's leadership from Columbia International University and is also a Licensed Massage Therapist. She is the proud wife of Stephen and the mother to three beautiful children, Leah, Ray and Shani. Her hobbies include running, pickleball, singing and spending quality time with her family. Her desire is to inspire others to know their worth in Jesus and to find their purpose in life through Him.

Follow Shani's Journey on Instagram @WALKER_ADOPTION

About the ILLUSTRATOR

SARA JO STARTED ILLUSTRATING books as a young girl. She would write short stories about her pets or the squirrels living in the attic and bring them to life with crayons. As Sara Jo grew, so did her love for painting, drawing, sewing, and creating with her hands. Being homeschooled on a Midwest farm meant she had lots of experience with her favorite furry subjects and more time to pursue her passion for art. It wasn't until she went to college that she got her first real art class. She went on to graduate with an art degree, and then taught art to school children, until she had her own. Sara Jo and her husband have two biological daughters and two daughters who were grafted into their family through adoption, both of which are blind. Now they homeschool their little women on their own Midwestern farm with 72 animals. They affectionately named this historic 1893 farmstead "Bryarton Farm." The bucolic views and peaceful setting are the perfect backdrop for Sara Jo to illustrate children's books as well as to teach her children.

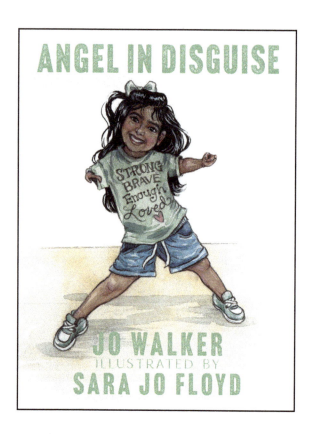

Shani Walker has more to share with you, her friends! Discover *Angel in Disguise*, the exciting second book about this extraordinary warrior princess. Learn all about disabilities and what it's like to be unique. Parents and children are given helpful insight into how we should treat those who may look different than us. Meet many of Shani's friends on the playground to see how we all have more in common than we may think. This uplifting resource gives families great conversation prompts to improve their interactions and understanding of individuals living with a disability, while encouraging those who were uniquely made by God to find their worth in Him.

Visit Amazon to find your copy of *Angel in Disguise*

Printed in the USA
CPSIA information can be obtained
at www.ICGtesting.com
LVHW071159140624
783125LV00003B/35